CAPITALISM AND NON ALIGNED SYSTEMS IN THE WORLD

MIGUEL JADIS

authorHOUSE®

AuthorHouse™
1663 Liberty Drive
Bloomington, IN 47403
www.authorhouse.com
Phone: 1-800-839-8640

First published by AuthorHouse 12/28/2013

ISBN: 978-1-4634-2174-8 (sc)
ISBN: 978-1-4634-2171-7 (hc)
ISBN: 978-1-4634-2170-0 (e)

Library of Congress Control Number: 2011910726

Printed in the United States of America

CONTENTS

ACKNOWLEDGEMENTS

Hereby, in primary of early product, of great and cordial thanks address to supporters and collaborators who encouraged and awaited impatiently the publication of this book:

My sincere thanks also extend to my Christian faith and co-workers.

This book is intended for the public, Christians and others who will draw better knowledge from it each day. For a pleasant and happy career, each reading will bring the salutary councils under the powerful glance of God; and a better comprehension of human motivations.

It's also a book with teaching and advisory value.

PROLOGUE

The universe depicts greatly a structural panorama of wonder which continuously leaves a very particular admiration to human beings to constantly accept the greatness and undeniable veracity of the living God to praise him.

The Master creates a distinctive and marvelous nature to represent him around the world. He treats each one by the same way; he gives the same right and duties to operate great things which should characterize him.

He is also that one which holds the breath of each individual and which fixes a special time to remove it without any interruption. In his infinite goodness, he made the expression of his faithfulness by giving the scientific pathways which accompany humans like temporal objects to show his magnificence, his glory and his incommensurable love.

As of the beginning, one says that the world was formed of a family, as it developed of number and run off the line between each member by division which the enemy has been established in order to better governing. Devil does it to avoid the members to join together to resolve their disagreements. It is thus a thrown into a panic attitude which degrades each family which does not want to maintain her responsibilities obtained from God. While feeling extremely the need for having a leader placed to take control of her rights and duties; that shows exactly the idleness.

The good sense should be in kind the subject of teaching to people to realize that is absolutely a renunciation and that the individual whom they want to take the load has the same responsibilities like them. The families which strip their benevolences resign of their responsibilities.

A leader is a nominated or elected person by a demography which charges to achieving a mission or a well defined work according to her will.

To have a leader or a group of people lead in various positions, it's like giving power to lead on them definitely. This employees always have the reasonable wages by formulating their own manner, either dictatorship or democracy. If the government establishes the dictatorship, the demography on what he exerts his power cannot express her will suitably. The practice of dictatorship is a powerful form which always uses ferocity to maintain people in squatting and they can pay the weight of imprisonment or even death. However, the operation of democracy is absolutely functioned with the liking of the demography which gives the employment. If there is omission, the people can to some extent remove that non functional government from the honorary employment.

With increasing of the human race, the world is surrounded by a multitude of systems heap up of various tendencies.

The Lord begins his world plan to the Jewish people which reject him, and which want to finally extend on the whole world his best system which unfortunately contains a minimal number which expresses the world contempt with his transcendental launching.

He wants to guide the men in obedience by his word to prove the intimacy and happiness of each individual to the divine framework in the course of this last time.

If human beings have their choice, God as Master and great creator can decide his will by giving the effective regulation during the last time.

One mentions that the human systems will lead to disappointment, but the one of God will lead to perfect happiness. The obviousness proves two destinations of two distinct extremes, and that the supreme hierarchy occupies by the Master and other hierarchy controls by the usurper who represents the opponents to global monarchy that established the Lord.

This explains why the world population is divided into two categories, and it receives orders coming from two different places.

A solemn recall is launched to all in order to avoid the fire which will blow soon, and this will take place everywhere to make an end to human beings; however, the wise ones will be saved.

Each population would make of better sound to establish the particular system to her liking. In the contrary case, a new provision would be liable to put in progress.

A new turning is being required urgently as essential facts for a manpower resulting in order to gain the best.

In fact to detach from the constant experiment which devalues the human race as a creature of glory?

It is an implication to maintain; that indicates the progressive development of a system which the demographic totality should emphasize.

After being splashed in the toxic mud, the baby needs somebody to take care of him, but an effective prescription should be applied in order to be disinfected!

A world tour to conquer!

CAPITALISM

There are capitalistic system and oligarchical capitalism:

The etymological aspect is powerful to teach and maintain by all explorers around the sphere to slow down the train of confusion which circumvents the whole world. That etymological rod is the essential force to be able to fight against precarious information on the rail of obviousness in fact to release human beings to review the transcendental exploration. Of this fact, the development of this topic is extremely important so as to make disappear all obscure forms which prevent the visibility to all.

If light ceases operating, the darkness will continue certainly to reign everywhere as the main power to lead towards the deep pit!

The topic 'capitalism' comes from Latin word capitalis of caput means having the maximum in manner of possession. The state invested in a way for drawing an income from individual or companies with a minimum rate. It can accumulate wealth in greater number while becoming richer; in a sense, it is thus devolution of wealth so that other ones can to some extent find a way in the progress path.

As long as runs the river, rejoice the ducks!

The capitalistic system or capitalism of state is imposed and functioned, but the people maintain the implication. The imposition of the state expresses that it gains the national funds and liquid to each company and individual of a respective value for a minimum rate. And also an interest rate for constructions, trade, agriculture and others, since the state works for the wellbeing of the population.

Indeed, this concept is better exerted to produce the maximum of all, encouraged each individual to take his responsibilities suitably. Let opening to each one the ways so as to gain his own fish. And this gives access to a great number of people to enrich by making possible the country to better progress. Those which understand the form make the weight by luminous research to practice the essential design in order to advance gradually.

A great and viable system which does not encourage idleness and that carries out the steps towards progress. That is a profit for the wealthier men of other countries to invest largely within the capitalistic framework. Work is a duty to maintain according to the divine orders. In a capitalistic country well structured, people who cannot work should support by state or temporary government, but those which do not want to work without cause of infirmity, suffer and do not take part in the race of progress.

Which collects the products without having sown the pips?

One is often crowned of joy during the harvest, even though the pain from the seed remains still in memory!

Somebody can be in the country and does not delight, if the direction of that individual is opposite to that of the country. One never invites the handicap to take part in a race which does not answer the necessary qualifications. One considers those which cannot play like observers of game. That implies that they do not take part in the national development. The plowman who works hard often has the necessary food for the bad seasons. When the lazy one sees the neighbor's interests he often complaints without having thought that he unfortunately made the choice of his experienced condition.

This structural formula contains all the national institutions and joints the ordering of almighty God while working hard or investing to create more jobs within territorial demography.

The capitalism is a better system between the human systems, because it encourages progress that is effectively the production of the suitable work!

Now, if the lazy ones do not want to work, they revolt against the Lord's order.

In fact, the capitalistic system does not require them to work, but God the Father.

Apostle Paul declares formally while saying: that which does not want to work, shows absolutely that he does not need to eat.

If many people are dissatisfied, they may call in judgment the great Creator.

Then, where the judgment will take place?

And who will be the judge?

Since the Master's order remains the same one; its up to the lazy ones to reconsider their careers to cease finally depositing their loads on the shoulders of the rich persons of the capitalism.

If the neighbor's meals annoys the nose of the lazy ones by its odorousness, they should change strategy in order to have a better career!

Indeed, the destiny of better living is to follow the direction of work which leads to prosperity!

"Manna was given in the wilderness as of antiquity" but today, if one goes and searches, one will find nothing. This is why, one must endeavor to work although it makes tiring, but the product is delicious; work makes free and thrives so as to integrate in the capitalistic system.

Let's not forget that destination is findable by following the suitable track!

Thus let us make haste today to avoid all forms of failure.

Demography is composed of two categories:

The state officials and the mass; the stripped class does not exist in the capitalism of state since everyone is working.

Those which are already on the top of the world pyramid encourage others to advance gradually to surely arrive beyond the concerned point which is a national and vital policy.

The capitalistic system contains indeed the functional state which raises all people from prospect to new prospect.

The functional aspect does not encourage idleness, but eliminates poverty in preference.

The state is the fundamental base of the capitalistic system which is composed of all the functional institutions through the country in order to meet the constant needs for the obvious demography such are:

The ministerial framework of health,

The ministerial framework of education,

The ministerial framework of justice,

The ministerial framework of security,

The ministerial framework of agriculture and commercial factors etc.

Systematic capitalism could be a framework definitively imposed by the state or the government in progress by a decree on all the demography of the country.

The state is basically the whole of all institutions that are well structured and established through the country in order to meet the constant needs of the vibrating demography.

All these fundamental bases must function fully and well balanced without distinction. Without the system of state, the country will be under flame of intense anarchy. As of the absence of the government the state continues to liquidate the services suitably. The state is not the government and is also not the people. Many underdeveloped territories are private essential points for the internal utility of the nation.

In developed countries, the state functions by the systematically established standards. It is the highest intense establishes within the population in a constant way for the good performance of these factors of which it is made up.

The capitalistic system contains three various categories which are:

1__the state

2__the wealthier men

3__the wealthy men

The state is the wealthiest that controls effectively the national institutions in the country and invests for the wellbeing of the population.

The wealthier men occupy the second position on the scale; they are the ones who create jobs within the population.

The wealthy men occupy the third position on the scale; they also create jobs through their enterprises. That's why in the capitalistic system there is no indigence.

Everyone should start using the power which one equips for his wellbeing!

The train will leave empty, if there is nobody to go on board!

In fact, one needs to stop blaming others for his own failure, but oneself!

TRANSITORY CAPITALISM

The transitory capitalism is a temporary governess establishes to better served the population. The government decides to restructure the precarious bases by making sure that each institution through the country functions a better way for a well defined period.

The government imposes the system to implement the current formula that failed to put in place by that new structural well balanced in order to avoid the worse. It would be the essential object for a way out of crisis in order to solve the situation during a short period; since it takes care of the good performance of all national institutions. If it would be necessary to take formal decisions to revoke and replace by his democratic authority in order to reinforce one or the national institutions for better serving the people.

Let's say that the government is placed in a temporary way although presides by an elected official of all territorial demography.

The government works in the state for the people. Since the nominees are placed in a temporary way, this important framework is necessarily required another person to succeed it for the governess of the institutions. In fact, the government is temporarily placed, but the state is permanently placed to serve the collective community through all the inhabited territory.

The elected hierarchy receives a specific mandate to supervise the good operation of the national institutions.

Politic, according to the world practice has two distinctive phases based on human actions:

A__ the positive aspect
B__ the negative aspect:

A__ the positive phase comes from Greek word politikè it is the whole of things concretely accomplished by the persons in charge for the wellbeing of the population. The functional politic consists in making more effective the national institutions that are contributed to the national progress.

It is a functional form without distinction through the territory; this implication is completely joining the etymological direction of democracy. This system includes all fundamental factors which form utility of each individual around the country; this topic should not utilize like a slogan for the profit of someone.

It is an excellent practice which illuminates all people in the geographical framework. That is the raison men who exert this politic entirely please the population which honor them and then entrust them the greater more. These people in kind may leave by death which prevents them, but their good works remain unforgettable in memory of these well-known. It is thus an exerted form which people or employers deserve.

One called it: 'Politic of life'

B__the negative phase comes from Latin word poly means several and tics means suckers; in full meaning: these are suckers of blood. The implication is that all elected or nominated people who do not have regard to their responsibilities while giving up the population in the drift. All factors of state do not function and the people are devoted to themselves. It is noted that this formula in the dictatorial countries the nation stuck in misery when the responsible people travel through the continents. This career is completely parallel to the functional democracy.

The candidates often employ soft words to carry them at the top of the coveted pyramid, but turn against the supporters, instead of concretizing their promises.

The parallel politic functions contrary, people await a direction while they go other direction; this indicates that they forget about them in the wilderness without help of a good Samaritan.

People face the howling lion, in a heat temperature, famished, without access of care, stuck in misery without being helped; it's like giving whip to someone to be punished. This negative formula is disappointing. Those which are victims of this hard career say that life is difficult, they do not understand absolutely by being unaware of reality.

The most important point is the method in function or the system in progress works against them. Since life is composed of soul and spirit according to the scientific topic of theology. The 2%, in opulence delight, the people suffer until dying in their partial poverty.

This negative one called: 'Politic of death'

All these principal institutions described form the state as utility for everyone. If the population can make the choice of his leaders, he can also decide his manner of living since he is sovereign. He will never make choice of dying, but living.

Many folks even think that this formula is an extension of the socialist system, but they cannot realize that democracy is the obvious exercise of the people which explains their right and duty and the state itself of its part works for the people. In a world people absolutely make the object of their responsibilities and the state itself has also its part. Democracy is the exercise of demography, the state works for the people which give the employment instead of different groups or different tribes among the population. The duty of the state is always working for the wellbeing of the population because it is the fundamental base which controls and the population maintains.

Never forget that the society forms of all demography of the panoramic phase thus inhabited, polyethnochromic or eider monoethnochromic.

A functional democracy includes the right and duty of each individual around the territory. It does not encourage laziness; but Communism does. Obviously, is very simple to realize that the people who work in the state are employees of the population who can instantly find their revocation based on their bad management. Knowledge is not a risk, but a brilliant light which guides the wise ones towards the path of happiness.

It's the most profound and functional form through the territory because the human being deserves these essential cares during the terrestrial career. The right to vote does not completely indicate the implication or the etymological of democracy. This form includes all basic elements which form utility of each individual in the national framework. It is an excellent implementation to protect each individual in the geographical map. A well structured system that leads towards national prosperity. This is why that the population achieves her civic duty to elect officials for various positions through the country in order to work as it is appropriate.

The transitory capitalism could be an obligatory framework by the government in progress by a decree on all the temporary country of manner to solve a serious situation or to maintain by the state for the good being of each individual in case the previous one failed. This rational system keeps everyone which forms the population under its shade.

The state officials impose, the population maintains the rule!

OLIGARCHICAL REGIME OR OLIGARCHICAL CAPITALISM

The oligarchical regime or oligarchical capitalism is a power which has a great influence in the government by the rich people that invest their wealth in election of many positions; they also invest to contractors who liquidate to the various actions which create jobs within the population to become richer. They are invisible, but they rule through the government that can not decide without their assent.

It is absolutely impossible to have the oligarchical regime and the capitalistic system, because they are not constituted by the same factors. That is why a country with that regime functions unbalance and depicts on the screen weakness view. They have to realize that they are two things which control the world those are: *wealth* and *power*; if someone has two things, one is qualified to control.

One must realize that nobody would like to collect the calabash for water melon since one normally invests to collect the fruits of his seed appropriately.

There are two facts to consider: either people invest whatever they can to enjoy their right or the wealthier men continue to have the sweet products of their seed. For this purpose, if the state wants to do something, it could control the interest of each individual of the particle indicated of the nominal area.

People themselves take loan by accepting the interest rate monthly or annual according the requirement of the investors. The state officials could intervene in case there is failure to cut off the questions by rules already established.

The state officials could place between the action and the individual to decrease the monthly payment by increasing the years or reformulating the contract to reduce the load.

The contractors themselves are the secondary axes which create jobs within the population. The officials may in fact establish the indicated rules to regulate the loans between the contractors and people who allocate the values according to the contents of the contract.

In the case of workers, the state officials have to employ many inspectors to supervise the treatment of people who work in independent industries to preventing that many people underwent ill treatment. Many of them resign to squat in the sad dead end, thinking that they do not have accessibility to get another job. And others suffer the effect of their chromic ornament in order to solve their problems. The work is a divine commands to obtain the daily bread, even through, industries are not a slavery places.

The owners of many industries are not the Master of the workers who often mistreat the weakened ones under their pressure.

The oligarchical or capitalistic regime forms of three categories which are:

1__the wealthiest men
2__the wealthier men
3__the wealthy men

The wealthiest men occupy the highest position on the scale and pump money in order to get more interest.

The wealthier ones occupy the second position on the scale that invest to make certainly their interest.

The wealthy men occupy the last position on the scale and create jobs just to gain their possible benefice.

These rich men create jobs by investing in the industries without the state and make it weak by their power. The capitalistic regime presents an unbalanced panorama.

Oligarchical capitalism is not the capitalistic system and it will never be!

Obviously, in order to have the capitalistic system, the most profound aspect one needs to know that the state must in fact control all the national institutions!

MYTHICAL CAPITALISM

Certain people are afraid that others do not reach or exceed their economic levels which would cause the suspension of work. Frankly, they do not need to have this faintness which would never arrive. This higher phase does not produce equality among the population as regards economy, but creating an increasing prospect like a rich country

As far as the workers obtain economic means as much as they spend.

As far as small capitalists progress the richer will be the great capitalists.

Never forget that the population itself develops in number and in age in a world which requires enough in all matters as pressure which requires constantly.

One hopes that this myth which occupies the thoughts of certain people will be disappeared to release them finally.

In the river runs water abundantly, but the mother is the source!

In addition, certain people think that the capitalistic system is bad; the problem is not the system, but they are the observers, because the system nevertheless prevents them going to school to learn a profession for a constructive career. The experiment proves already that the absence of knowledge is the leading cause of poverty which devastates them.

Considering evolution which challenges the world in the last dispensation, if many people do not prepare to face the gradual aspects of science, worse will be their situation for being excluded themselves from the race of progress.

One must remember that destination is always reached while following the true path which leads to it.

If the doors are widely opened, then one makes the choice not to put aboard, one cannot hope for the best.

May this description help finally to gain the rail of prosperity.

It is true that gold comes from the earth, but it is necessary to dig and dig until the discovery!

NON ALIGNED SYSTEMS IN THE WORLD

The non aligned systems of the world are the following:

A__GLOBAL MONARCHY

B__SOCIO MONARCHICAL

C__SOCIO DICTATORIAL

D__COMMUNISM

E__ SOCIALISM

GLOBAL MONARCHY IN THE LAST DISPENSATION

The topic Monarchy comes from Greek language, is composed of monos means single or power of one and archos means law or rule; in a word, it is a power controls by a king who exerts his supreme authority on the demographic face which he reigns. Nobody can resist is decisions, he is only dominated on the circumference of his geographical land. Within the framework of Jesus, it is a transcendental and incomparable system because he is the redeemer and also one of the creators who operate marvelous things. The creation is also created by him and he is worthy to be honored for the salvation works under authorization of God the Master.

This new formula highlighted at the end of times, Matthew 3: 17 by the angel Gabriel according to what reports Luke 1: 26-38 and Matthew 1: 18-23 which is the achievement of the Isaiah's prophecy 7: 14-16. And of the mysterious operation of the Spirit concerning the birth of the Messiah while was born in Bethlehem. There was a demonstration of many Angels in one alternative praised the Father for splendid works that certainly many people verified.

The world received a mysterious visit for the first time which could be a pride not only to the Jews of which was occurred in what attracted the incarnated creator, and also to all around the global planet. His eternal power, his marvelous name, his missionary work and his divinity remain undeniable. Subsequently, all other prophets received the favor to communicate the intention of the Lord. In spite of all posterior prophecies, God, with wonder decides to send his only son Jesus, the first born of all creation. His beloved son brings in this perverse world a new method, a new contrary message to the patriarchate and the Judaism which were the two fundamental aspects of the theocratic system. This last page has been based on spiritual factors in order to deliver the souls of the human beings from all tricks of the great usurper.

God allowed Moses to mention this visit that badly accommodated by certain people who must be the plenitude of divinity for all human ones created with his image. He took the human shape to achieve a special mission; the obvious intervention of angels and preparations during his glorious appearance which proved the complete vibration of the celestial corpses. It was thus an extreme advantage for whole humanity to have him at present on the earth.

All God's prophets that preceded the gracious period of the Messiah, obtained from him the authorization to announce with exactitude his message. They were simple men that the Lord chose to achieve extraordinary things. They were subjugated to sins, to death and they also had access to rights and duties.

During the last time, Lord sends his son Jesus, the first of creative works to bring good news to humanity.

He was impeccable which explains that he was not subjugated to sins and death. He had not had any heritage with human beings, this is why he declares:

"The birds have nests to rest, but I do not have a place to rest a little"

The last prophet has a message of eternal life for each individual through all corners of the earth.

And he exclaims repentance to the mankind, because the kingdom of heaven is approached, that indicating to put on the way of preparation to become member of his spiritual church in order to obtain the eternal kingdom of the living God. It was a badly accommodated message of his people; still he declares: come to me, all you who labor and are heavy laden and I will give you rest, meaning salvation for the souls while following his transcended instructions. He raised deaths, he cured the sick people and he fed the poor people. His right was eating and drinking, he did not have a woman and child. His message has been a complete package which centered on the spiritual base guided by the glorious Spirit according to Apostle Paul, Galatians 5: 22.

By promulgating the Gospel of freedom in parallel to the commands of men, traditions, patriarchal and judaical facts, causing the rising of the priests and the followers of the old formulas which by man occasions try to lapidate Jesus, but he often escapes. The men of truth have always those of lie as enemies.

The various operations of these people to get rid of the Messiah is to kill Jesus in order to maintain the same practices, the transitory things, the buckled influence which push them to put hand on him like criminal to execute the plan of the crafty usurper.

HIS HUMAN CAREER

The shedding of blood has been the value of the disobedience that God at the beginning prescribed as sacrifice of animals for the humans according to Leviticus fourth. Therefore, the bloodshed has been established for forgiveness of sins. Author of epistle to Hebrews denotes on chapter tenth the fourth verse chapter 10: 4, that the blood of animals was impossible to remove the sins and to make pure the man's conscience. The lovely God changes the plan by giving grace to save human beings from their impeccability which was a profitable way for devil to disappear the human race on the surface of the earth. By his omniscience, he has been announced the setting up of the last structure in order to deviate the devil's plan to save the human race.

God shows his love while designating his son to pay for the burden of humanity which abandons voluntarily his glory in the heaven to live in the earth and to be mistreated by many people. At that time, the high priests of God among the Jews were unhappy and stood against him during his earthly career.

His mission was prescribed by God to implement the salvation of humans as the last plan to save them from destruction which will take place soon. By acknowledging the truth and grace to all, the best form by taking position of the sinners through all corners of the earth in order to pay the debt of humanity. Parallelisms treat him like good-for-nothing while saying: he is the son of Joseph the carpenter, Nazarene "nothing better could come from this known suburb" people look on appearance, but the foolish ones can not realize that the Master often utilizes the ordinary men to achieve extraordinary things, and worthless things of this world in marvelous things to make burst his glory.

One day, Jesus attentively looks at those which are held around him while saying: "People of this world, what do they want? They are as children who ask for music which do not dance; the Lord gives them John the-Baptist who lives in the mountain, he does not eat and does not drink with them, they treat him like demon. The son of God comes, he eats and drinks with them, they call him great eater and drinker; the men do not know what they want" the experiment proves the obviousness, the similar people which one gives assistance today are the first ones to be supervised because they often give the first blows. The unwise ones are always the victims. It is impossible to record all the painful facts, but God has all of them in memory. "He declares that animals in spite of their incapacities exert sometimes gratitude towards their benefactors, but the human beings act differently.

His transcendental mission in the world unmasks the wise ones of all forms of ignorance like the light of the world to facilitate the entry of the paradisiacal place. He gives the gospel as only food necessary to the souls of men of good will, a defensive and offensive tool. Other components which form the spiritual and powerful armor in order to continue the battle of the last time are greater than human ones. Many people see that their interests do not find in this new formula, work against him so as to destroy all elements of bases.

This mission was the priority aspect during his terrestrial race. A corrupted system does not need righteous people for fear that its actions might be revealed and denounced. Despite everything, Jesus accomplishes a partial of his mission, and he continues his glorious work.

One charges him to have claimed to be the son of the living God, the King of the Jews which can destroy the temple and to rebuild it in three days. The enemy always uses trap to destroy that which he believes being his adversary, a practice that many people are always useful. Sometimes the source of interest appears tasty, but the fundamental base is the permission. Despite everything, they interest to exterminate him on the surface of the earth in order to continue in darkness.

When the moment came, they arrested him and took him along to be judged as a criminal; a weak creature which dared to judge the Creator.

What a deviation!

Of which judgment has he undergone, the son of living God? And which was his defender?

Which is dared to make the judgment of that which created him?

The high priests were the first enemies of Jesus that lead him to death. The chapter ninth of John's book presents one of the reactions of these men that delivered Jesus the powerful Savior of the world to be mistreated. One drove a crown of thorns on his head, his blood was shed for the sins of the humans, one nailed him like criminal on the cross, he exhaled Mark 15: 37; Luke 23: 46; John 19: 30; Matthew 27: 50; as proof, one buried him. Paul declares that Jesus was ready to take death for humanity, Romans 5: 6 and to give life. He declares: I am the way, the truth and life. Now, the men have not to pay, that is why the Christians must be delighted of such privilege in Jesus Christ and that will see him soon face-to-face; he lives everlasting to everlasting because the earth could not keep him. He is the living redeemer that gives the eternal redemption to the believers.

His death was it thus a deliverance to deviate the plan of the almighty God which is the Master?

This is why these people cannot see in Jesus divinity and power when he took part of the Malchus ear and place it like before.

Time that he passes on the earth after death is definitively a victory for the valiant ones of the ceaseless revolution which will lead to eternal happiness.

The Jews should be able to realize that they were acted dishonestly in order to repent. In preference, they declared that the partisans of the defunct come to conceal him during the night while the guards fell in deep sleep.

His death accomplished a part of the mission; he took what humanity had deserved in order to give life abundantly once at all, offered himself to give access in the spiritual and eternal sanctuary. While abolishing the act of the Old Testament to establish in forced the New Testament which is the better one.

How were the entrails of these malicious which struck him?

How were the entrails of those which inserted the crown of spines braided in his head?

How were the entrails of those which nailed him on the cross?

And those which were followed far the scene?

He was resurrected from death which was a conclusive proof and a tangible victory for the believers. His resurrection was announced to the disciples, according to Matthew 16: 21; 20: 19; Luke 9: 22; 18: 31; 24: 7; Mark 8: 31; 9: 31; 10: 33; Luke 24: 6. In spite of surveillance of the guards, the Lord God revived his beloved son among deaths, the stone rolled and the earth shook, the power of Satan could not prevent him, the angel of the eternal God declared the fact, Matthew 28: 5-7. The apostle Paul gave the confirmation to the Christians of Corinth the first book of the chapter fifteenth reassuring them of his resurrection after death.

He lived forty days on the earth which should be a sign for the enemies to think about their actions that drove to death Jesus the wonderful redeemer. He spoke about his ascension toward the Father and consolidated the disciples to be delighted for having the excellent promise, John 14: 1-2. The theological instruction is absolutely a necessary basis that shows the characters of the real God to better serving him, the source of all new spiritual perspectives for the new creature.

During his time on the earth, the miracles that he performed should be a way to glorify him to confide him, to obey him and to hope always on him as the only overseer of souls. One is surrounded of his eternal power, his immense love, his marvelous work, his incomparable history and glorious presence. He referred this quick declaration to the disciples of this moment by saying: if someone serves me and follows me, where I am, he will be also, John 12: 26.

The malicious ones celebrate their cruel acts, but they are always screaming of their turn!

His departure mentioned by Luke one of the servants of God in chapter 24 the following verses 50-53. On the way which leads to Bethany, he was accompanied by his disciples; that being the last seconds of the departure towards his Father. He encouraged them to maintain their firm conviction and he pointed out the promise of the eternal life by showing the importance of his departure.

While they stood there, looking the departure of the Savior and wonderful friend in the cloud then appeared two angels of the Lord reminded them of Jesus's promise in John fourteenth while saying: "He will come back the same way as one sees him depart to the heaven. This confirmation assured the disciples the time of Jesus and also all Christians of today until the removal."

Apostle Paul reassured on what the Christians of this dispensation the certainty of their honorary integration in this vital kingdom. His departure watched by the followers, where he was before and the disciples were comforted by an angel who told them: he will come back in the same way of which one sees him going up. The short period that the purchased of Christ have to pass in the world can not compare to the one of eternity. Sometimes, they even expose in the flesh, but calling to stay unshakable by the almighty Lord. If there was not this heavenly hope, this painful moment in the disturbed world would be the unfortunate destiny for everyone, but one is crowned of his constant presence under the guidance of the Holy Spirit one is often comforted of his marvelous promise, Ephesians 4: 30.

The presence of the Holy Spirit of which absolutely will ensure his absence like marks important and foundation of the world kingdom or global system which will be handed during his nomination, and he blessed them. Then Jesus went away in his place like beforehand announced.

The servant Luke denoted in detailed manner concerning the spiritual kingdom of Christ Jesus by operation of the Holy Spirit based on the gospel at the designated time according to the Lord after his ascension in Acts second chapter.

The power of Jesus does not exert on all people around the world. The Christians are the only ones through the terrestrial planet who practice his gospel, doctrine which gives the eternal life. It is the last means established by his arrival to save humanity. This last formula is parallel with the primitive time. The son of God reigns on those which receive Holy Spirit. His spiritual kingdom bases on profitable works of the glorious Spirit; a fractional number estimating that 8% of the world population, therefore, there is an unbalance in the human race. Many people would like better to go to paradise without implementing the basic elements which conform to the established standards that the Savior claims.

According to his promise, all those which are the object to practice his doctrine, he will come to take them soon for their eternal reward. His law remains until his eminent apparition, the effective tool, nutritive phase, a prevention to avoid the eternal punishment. The gospel is like a special prescription to treat the sick people and defensive and offensive weapons for the regeneration of the devoted men.

The promise of the glorious Spirit for the baptism of the apostles at the day of Pentecost, but the same Holy Spirit as promised comes and lives in the hearts of the believers which receive him to ensure their membership in the spiritual kingdom of Jesus, the son of the living God.

The son of the living God is the "King of the global kingdom on which he always imposes, but he is not the King of a particular nation."

A negative impact extends on the world scale by blooming of a multiple churches which deny the existence of Holy Spirit like trainer of the believers. At the shore of the ocean, people of various congregations are held while shouting: we will cross the sea easily to conquer and enjoy happiness forever. However, they refuse the means of transport which are available to them.

Can they fly away? Absolutely not!

Still, they await that one which can nothing do for oneself and even them.

The usurper tries still even after the departure of the Messiah to extend the dense fog around the world to blind completely his workmen. He fills their hearts with all deceptive elements in order to have them and take them along to his liking. He lied, while informing the angels which were with him in the heaven of which was going to divide the kingdom of God, unfortunately, the devil and his allies would not manage to resist the Master, their place was not any more in the celestial place.

Again, he lied just after creation to the first parents. Causing a multitude of sins invade the screen of the terrestrial sphere, because the influence of sins leads certainly human beings to become his workmen in order to lead them to eternal disappointment.

Humans are misled by believing that the death of Jesus was a means to prevent the work of almighty God. Who made the choice of special people which were to be able to show the face of the celestial divinity to other people of terrestrial planet, instead they go against the commands of the Master.

THE WORLD MISSION, FAVOR REJECTED

In a chronological way one cannot evaluate since the period of the Abraham patriarch until the day of the great opening of salvation to other nations. So, all people should be delighted by having access to salvation in Christ Jesus. He received the full authority from God to operate as King on the whole world, Matthew 28: 19. It is recommended to all men to obey him, Matthew 17: 5. Moses made the prediction of this glorious history to all men in all places to listen to him, Deuteronomy 18: 18. It seems that the legitimate children do not want to always recognize all benefits they have from their parents, but the ones of the concubine do. This nation received an honorable access, unfortunately, it denied her celestial privilege by declaring that it's still waiting for the Messiah who has to come; however, other nations have been unceasingly celebrated to have let enter to the global system or spiritual kingdom of Jesus Christ.

He sought to establish a perfect relation with these people by giving firstly the patriarchate to which these people did not feel comfortable to maintain; and that abolished God, secondly the Judaism which it rejected completely and thirdly Christianity that it also rejected, the very last plan to which it could to some extent find the eternal happiness.

Usually, the granted favor is not appreciated; even the commands punishes the transgressors severely!

One wonders: what do the human beings want? The beforehand selected people reject their paramount part and other people themselves refuse this great favor.

Still, this salvation and world mission remain an abandoned work.

He offered himself like one of the Creators, Savior, Redeemer, King, brother, friend and lawyer etc; the men prefer their own kind, animals and things. Jesus offers his kingdom or world religion; they prefer instead the muddled systems of the world. The Master gives his Gospel as the world law humans choose in preference the confused ideologies which make suffering unceasingly.

They are calling to love God and their neighbor, they prefer in essence to function in enmity with God the Master and hate instead their neighbors. Finally, the latter reject paradise which they may be able to obtain by faith in Jesus Christ, and they make finally the choice of hell, place of ceaseless torment instead of paradise.

If the last minutes could be sufficient in case which humanity decides to achieve this transcendental mission, it will gain the rail of her destiny as it is appropriate; again all remain uncertainty.

The patient rejected the drug that the doctor prescribed to be restored!

WHICH ARE INDEED GOD'S PEOPLE IN THIS LAST DISPENSATION?

The best moment has arrived to highlight all bonds which leave to know our being and our future to which each one remains to attach, from which and why our dependence; so many filled of temporal blessings and especially the spiritual ones to join that the heavenly Father claims absolutely.

The last dispensation in which humanity rests now, leaves to contempt men in preference of the things of the world which disturb constantly. The promise of eternal God to all nations continues progressively as it is appropriate; but it remains to humanity to be put at the research of the source, nature, goal and the rules which are the continual phase as regards the application.

The accounts of the book of Genesis depict the beginning of all and give exactly the declarations which scatter in the verses which follow: Genesis 18: 18; 22: 18; 14: 49; 26: 4.

The great Creator mentions the first formula while speaking about the patriarchal religion. A retrospective glance is the guaranteeing fundamental to each one to explore finally this transcendental reality.

After the failure of Babel's tower followed the flood, the loving God addresses to Abraham of the posterity of shem, one of son of Noah, while saying: "In you, all nations of the earth will be blessed" Implying the salvation of the men comes from God by the posterity of Abraham while speaking about Jesus making flesh or incarnated, it is what concretizes in Acts 15: 14; 17: 30; and recalling by Jesus himself, John 3: 16. This determines that the sins of mankind move him away from the Lord. The provisions of the two former formulas were not effective; that is why, that he judged to grant grace to the sinners in the whole world, the last by the presence of his beloved son, Jesus.

The rejection of Jesus by many Jews is a revolt against the strict order of God, John 1: 11-13; 5: 46-47; 9: 28. Like mediator, he occupies the central position to restore the reconciliation between God and human beings by implementation of a new structure based on spiritual points which are eternal.

Apostle Paul declared this: this great privilege is initially announced to the Jews firstly, but they push back, and that they consider themselves unworthy of the eternal life. Then, he turns towards the pagan ones since the promise is also to them who receive this plan of redemption ardently that the Master of all promised, Acts 13: 46.

Indeed, he sends the apostles through the world, Matthew 28: 19.

Luke reveals the last declaration of Jesus to his disciples before his departure towards his Father, Acts 1: 8.

The mission of Jesus is a world work, guided by Holy Spirit to make possible this splendid mission (the good news of salvation) by the single means which is to answer the transcendental call of Jesus, Matthew 11: 28-29 so that spreads Holy Spirit, Ephesians 1: 13-14.

To those which obey the Gospel like only rule to follow as of the beginning until removal, he ensures the transition of same works to transform them for their eternal life. Therefore, without the presence of Holy Spirit, it's impossible to be called God's people. It is requested to whole humanity to imitate Jesus through his gospel in order to be pleased to God the great Creator, John 14: 15; 15: 14. He received the Christ title comes from the Greek word holy Christos meaning, put separately and by his works. In other hand, all the followers themselves receive their title as Christians derived from Greek word christianos means setting a part for God and must walk as he went himself to implement all things which characterize God the Father. All Christians who respectively maintain their part in the kingdom of Jesus form God's people or ambassadors around the world.

Today, they function under the dictation of the Holy Spirit in order to be transformed to join necessary qualities of the Master. Their part in the spiritual kingdom is to maintain the bonds relative which characterize Jesus, the savior in whom they find eternal redemption. They are holy people separated from other people of the world by the new order which begins with the presence of the Messiah approximately year 33.

True God and Master of this total distinctive creature gave his transcendental truth and revealed to all to unmask of veil so that there is only one flock for the overseer of souls.

Therefore, the wise ones always heap up of happiness, but misfortune remains in the rebels' house!

CHARACTERISTIC FACTS OF GOD'S PEOPLE

The factors which characterize God's people are the following: love, joy, peace, patience, kindness, goodness faithfulness, gentleness and self-control. All these relative elements make possible by Holy Spirit, the special correspondent of glorious God.

He ensures the transition from devoted kingdom of Satan to the kingdom of Jesus Christ; each continent can have one or more. The new birth of the believers is ensured by a perfect career which directs towards the pathway of eternal happiness.

They are in perfect communion and nourish of the same nutritive elements by the same wonderful Spirit. They carry the title of their powerful King; they have the same belief, the same feeling, the same heart, the same hope and the same thoughts, Philippians 2: 2.

The dogma or the fundamental base of this kingdom is salvation by preaching the gospel of Jesus Christ. Apostle Paul was the most powerful tool of the primitive time and he was also the central subject of this work missionary work, since the world was not filled yet of an huge crowd; he declared as follows: "the gospel has to preach to all creation" the most important point is the growth to nourish its production all the men in all places. Apostle John reaffirms while saying: "Whoever goes further and does not remain in the doctrine of Christ does not have God, but that which remains in this doctrine has the Father and the son while speaking about Jesus, 2 John 9. And then he adds this, if somebody comes to you and this doctrine do not bring, do not receive him in your house, and not even greeting him, 2 John 10"

The Christians are ambassadors of God on all the extent of the earth to defend their special mission, the heaven is their fatherland. The Christians conform to the invaluable basic qualifications by the Spirit of glory which the Lord had sent.

Which are the people such filled the requirements to call themselves God's people?

That the wise individual dares to give these people since the Lord uses a new formula in the gospel of his son without mixture.

One hopes that this chapter will employ as torch to enlighten all men on the surface of the earth in order to cease travelling in immense delusion to see from now on the shining splendor of wonderful God.

To be conformed to that requests of the Master, one needs the following points:

A __To believe in the same way
B__To accomplish 5 steps that gives access to conversion or salvation
C__To receive and maintain the Spirit for the transformation, resurrection and celestial departure

D__To worship the same manner

E__To carry a title relative to that of the King

F__To maintain the gospel like only law of practice without mixture

G__To have the same hope

H__To have the characteristic marks of Jesus

I__ To know that the kingdom of Jesus Christ is spiritual

J__And to have perseverance

A royal structure of the new formula is distinctive to the old formulas concerning a well determined nation, but the latter extending around the world. That is why, the Savior sends the apostles by declaring as follows: "Conversion of humans in order to be saved of this perverse world which soon will destroy and all what it contains" After the selection of the apostles, other people who come to Jesus answer the call launched in Matthew 11: 28-29.

All nations of the earth can in fact obtain salvation while answering the solemn appeal of Jesus. The apostles preached the gospel of Jesus Christ and the enthusiastic Christians continue that evangelical works until the last hour which thus will precede the removal of glorious and incomparable church or the global kingdom by the living redeemer. Now, God formally gives the favor to all men of the earth to form the people which belong to him. The old formula is null and voided and made place to the new and better one which has been in force. Nobody dares to use the abolished phases or the ministry of death one which produces curses unceasingly and even death to people who disturb of good sense.

Lastly, all those which conform to these requisitions of glorious Savior form God's people.

Attention to the stiff neck!

Any expired prescription which is the subject of using becomes automatically a violent poison to destroy, but not to cure!

Beforehand, this same drug was effective for a good treatment, but, when it is expired, produced opposite and even death,

In a word, the old form is null and void. The new form is in force until the removal of the elected ones of Christ who will produce finally eternal life for the enthusiastic servants.

Many people think that God has a special nation; however, that population has been denied Jesus the Messiah of the world. The best opportunity is given to the world to rethink in what attracted the people of God!

Following normally the Master's steps is effectively the sign of obedience!

THIS KING, IS HE TRULY GOD AS CERTAIN PEOPLE BELIEVE IN THE WORLD?

The reliable information on the topic God could to some extent help in etymological phase so as to find resolutely the obviousness sustained. And by using the theological phase, one can finally provide the truth like a conquest given up a long time, now reviewing research to enlighten the men indistinctly. Since Lord is the truth, he established to human to get away from darkness which blinds their intelligence in order not to see shining the splendor and glory of the true God on the surface of the earth.

The word 'Theos' comes from the Greek language, meaning God the being not created, existed by himself, that which does not have a beginning and the end, that which does not give his glory to anyone else.

He has a very particular veneration and he also has various appellations such are the following ones: YHVH a quotation without vowel which becomes later Yahvé means Eternal; Elohim means strong, powerful God; Yahvé Jiré means God will provide; Yahvé Rapha means Eternal who cures you; Yahvé Nissi means the Eternal my banner; Yahvé Schalom means Eternal of peace; Yahvé Raah means Eternal my shepherd; Yahvé Tsidkenu means Eternal is right; El-Schaddai means God the Almighty; El Elion means very high God; El Olam means God of eternity; El Ganna means God is vigilant; El Hai means alive God; Adoni means Lord.

Unfortunately, many religions use the word Jehovah like a name allotted to God and that makes the act of practice of the lazy men around the terrestrial planet.

The religions which open out easily among men around the world do worst things to unconverted people than good by division and their precarious and destructive informations.

And the members throw deeply in the most intense confusion which lets see that there is no possible way to be withdrawn thereupon.

Now, it comes the moment to meet and to maintain the truth as light to guide towards the pathway of incomparable happiness. A retrospective glance could take us along far in antiquity to collect the fundamental factors to understand and accept the present and future events which must arrive soon. The obvious points are sufficient to give the relative information as regards reality.

The book of the beginning revealed Jesus like one of the Creators, Genesis 1: 26-27.

Holy Spirit affirms that Jesus is the first created in the heaven by God the Master, Colossians 1: 15. And reveals that all visible and invisible things were created by him.

Many prophets announce the arrival of Jesus the son of God who will make missionary work of the last plan for the salvation of whole humanity since he swears not to destroy by water anymore, but fire.

The great and sincere expressions show the incommensurable love of the Lord for this marvelous creature according to his image.

Jesus is the first created by God the father which is the great Creator. He sent him on the cursed world to be able to pay the ransom of perverse humanity. He voluntarily gives up his glory in the celestial place.

The name of Jesus has the highest meaning than all other names, meaning savior, he also has Emmanuel as nickname which means God is with us, because he is sent by the Lord for a special mission. The definite word Christ is the attribution of his missionary work on all the extent of the earth.

God calls him son according to verse sixteenth chapter three of the book of John.

He has fully authorization to do all for the glory of God according to these following mentions, John 3: 35; 5: 32; 17: 2; Matthew 11: 27; 28: 18; Luke 10: 32; Hebrews 2: 8.

When he was baptized, his divine nature and his human nature were recognized by many folks, the Holy Spirit arised in shape of dove and God was made hear in these words: this one is my beloved son in which I put all my affection, Matthew 3: 17.

He prays the Father to guide the believers in a perfect unity which can make possible by the transformation of Holy Spirit; he declares while saying: the Father and I, we are one, which means their intimacy.

Many people believe that there exist three God; it is absolutely absurd to believe and teach that way.

The graphic phase is this: God takes his decision to save humanity in his incommensurable love; he gives the load to Jesus Christ and Holy Spirit to carry out his part of that marvelous plan.

He sends Jesus Christ for the redemption of human beings, Jesus obeys and implements this marvelous mission according to his intention.

God, the Master sends Holy Spirit for a salvation mission; he obeys and implements the partial of the marvelous mission according to the will of the almighty Father.

There exists only one God who decides and divided the plan in two fundamental fragments, partial carried out by Jesus Christ and other partial implements by Holy Spirit, together they achieve a common work or they arrive at a common solution to the liking of the Master which is the salvation of men, Ephesians 4: 6; 1 Timothy 2: 5; John 17: 3; Galatians 3: 20.

Jesus declares: that which sees me, also sees my Father because he sent me

And he spoke about the Holy Spirit that God will send for the salvation of repurchased ones.

Illustration: a father who sends his son to exert a specific mission elsewhere, obviously, he has mandated or authorized to put in execution this invaluable work. If one receives him perfectly, one also receives that which sent him, but if some rejects, one also rejects that one by which he was sent.

At the time of the nomination of Jesus as King, God declares this: "Your throne, O God, is eternal; the scepter of your reign is a scepter of equity; you love justice and you have hated iniquity. That is why, O God, your God has you anointed of an oil of joy above your equal. You, Lord, you have at the beginning founded the earth and the heaven which are the work of your hands"

Notification: The Lord raises him of his obedience and of his fidelity to the redemptive tasks. However, his missionary work still continues, while interceding in favor of the elected officials in heaven and soon under authorization of God, he will appear in the cloud to take the faithful servants, last phase of the achievement of his transcendental mission.

It's like a king in intimacy honors his beloved son under the terms of his obedience calls him while saying: "My King" by his affection.

To retain this well, God gives various names to son of the morning such as: devil, Satan, dragon, old snake because of his bad attitudes although he is also created by him.

This vibrating revelation is a dazzling phase for all these which are put in the search of reality in order to be delighted. In spite of dense ignorance, the truth never ceases nourishing the untiring explorers.

In appropriated way:

Jesus was not God!

He is not God!

And he will never be!

But he is certainly one of the creators;

And the first creative work of the true God.

Thus, all his power emanate of God.

By maintaining his obedience, his faithfulness and intimacy or agreement with the Master, that is why, he declares as follows: the Father and I, we are one.

It is necessary to comply with the etymological rule which exist between the words "son and Father" which indistinctly gain their essential functions to world teaching to nourish the teachers and students of this reality to delight.

"Finally, one must realize that the great Creator wants that all men arrive at the knowledge of truth for their salvation."

SOCIO MONARCHICAL

This theme Socio monarchical combined of socio derived of society and monos from the Greek word means single or only one and archos from Greek word means law or rule. It is sovereignty or supreme power placed as king or head of the kingdom which exerts his power absolutely, it's a system controls by a king and which continues by the royal family in case one passes away. The authorities which operate under his dictation observe only all the ordinances. His domination remains during his entire human race like heritage.

The king has power to take away life or leave in life and to destroy the ones which refuse to express his will, the royal decisions are irrevocable, and nobody is authorized to contradict. The king commands, people obey and his sovereignty remains until death.

On the top of the pyramid rests the magnificence of people of the amusing kingdom which rejoices the first fresh dew. The population that overpowered under the sun, smiles while saying: the members of the royal family look like angels, their faces are like diamond lately arrived, and their cloths are like prepared from an unknown planet.

This formula covers partial of the world, many guys think of leaving this career which prevents them from being able to integrate so as to taste the flavor, because experiment is better and what should be the subject of their dream.

Illustration: A child asks his mother: when will be our turn in the kingdom to control? His mom asks him: are you insane? The child answers his mother: why? She says: you have a bad intention which can take you along to death, because this power is a familiar heritage; my child keeps silent for better spending your days in peace. In insistence he declares: that indicates that our family was born to live in this manner until death, and mama says: yes!

The child continues to talk by saying: I surely think that people go school to become whatever they want to become, but never think of this impossible nobility place. And he quotes: I hope to see the invisible person who made the choice of this particular family to explain me about this national imbalance which rejects the 97% of the population to the profit of 3%! No! Thousand times no! It is not possible, if the state is a vital system establishes for everyone in the country to which they have to take active so transmissible part, and the beauty of people of the territory remains the same one.

Many people do not have any problem to accept as long the system provided facilities and can even think that the system is the best. So they are always amusing, defending and contemplating the movement of the monarchical system which surrounds them continuously; despite everything, they don't need absolutely any glasses for better seeing.

The gentles refuse the visibility which makes discover the microbes which remain deeply in their hands which may in fact cause fear to use them in their mouths!

Their prospect does not arrive on the scale evolution, as of their birth until their death and that the cheer reviews their repetition. Honoring and supporting the system constantly.

Finally their choice is parallel to that of the small child, and is not an exposure. Because the lion never lets swallow by hare! That which wants his days prolonged exposing never, but that which exposes the fact for him and other that he opened their eyes. He may not enjoy long years his effort, other ones do, and they are often called the infallible man 'Hero.'

This formula exerts simultaneously with global monarchy, because the Master wanted as well as only one system extends on all the earth and that Jesus his son as the King. This indicates a failure system that will finally cease existing soon since God does not speak about another one.

Indeed, the socio monarchical is an absolutely opposite system to global monarchy and other systems around the world which contain the distinctive elements.

The royal candy stimulates appetite to fatten, but its powerful effect blinds intelligence!

SOCIO DICTATORIAL

The socio dictatorial or the autocratic system is the wild act imposed coming from an elected official or nominee on the population which unfortunately awaits the best from him. It is a mode which controls in all forms to maintain the exercise of the dictatorship on the people; there are two things to consider here, "the will of each individual and the dictatorship of the government" Only the etymological aspect or the practice could to some extent help to obtain the importance which claims the grammatical and suitable order. Because missing the real context produces ignorance, the immense ocean where are regrettably deaths in great number.

The population has to obey, not being able to retort the government commands. This is why that the countries provided this formula retain captive people until death. It is easy to say to others to practice the law, when the leaders themselves are excluded. Such to others are in great number, but as to them nothing exists.

They love to be on power; daytime they exert their manner,

nighttime they think so as to increase more rules on the population. People of these governments are condemned to act according to the dictation of their chiefs. They cannot express their will as well, but those of the dictatorial which govern. If the great Creator gives will to humans, why are they detached from this privilege?

So the socio dictatorial by more the sharp actions mean system tallied established by somebody to endeavor the people to exert it, which indicates that people are under the dictation of somebody who controls. This form which is placed easily destroyed the independence of territorial demography and is a formula of slavery to attract on him the glances of all like the powerful whole. He pronounced his words strongly, and the people must have the ears largely opened to hear and obey without contradicting. Mostly of the time, the saved ones of this gangrene are deaths. The living ones ask constantly, when will it be the day of their decease?

What everyone must know, when one cannot express what one wants, it is a boundary, from or a form of slavery, on this, one obtains the obviousness. In obviousness, it is a system to be avoided, because this system makes suffering the entire human race.

This screen is badly seen by the victims, but well by the sensualists.

The escaped prisoners can find death if they are found by the government.

The socio dictatorial is really a wild and timorous formula that partial of the earth undergoes its effect unfortunately. People are waiting these leaders which do not care about them, they may wish that someone comes to shake the ground by a tremor of high voltage for a total deliverance.

People would say: when will come the day of their release?

The bad experiments remain vital in the memory, but the deliverance itself is always happiness coming from revolting of brave conquerors.

If the way of living is the honor, this honor is already absorbed in the abyss. A new book of dictionary would write to place the words in the grammatical order, and then the word honor will give its opinion as it is appropriate and than the topic dishonor will regain its place too. The great Creator teaches human beings to recognize their own kind and to harmonize themselves suitably according to his intention. He wanted as this marvelous creature to enjoy his splendor, his infinite love and his power continuously through the authentic world.

This non literal formula according to the etymological way remains in the thoughts of certain men spread everywhere like a practice, violating the divine requisition and human right in substantial factors.

This system is also parallel to global monarchy in substances contained.

The fat duck screams, the babies tremble!

SOCIALISM

The etymological aspect of the topic 'socialism' comes from Latin word <u>socialis</u> derived of society.

Socialism or socialist system is the fundamental exercise of state for the people. A system places to serving all the population in the same manner or of the same sight without distinction; from the point of view of health, education, justice, safety and economy etc.

On level of government, people can elect and re-elect officials at various governmental stations to regulate the fundamental businesses for the well being of the country and can replace according to the will of the population for a well defined reason. They have access to vote and to even present for any stations in elections of the country. Many people are able to have their own commercial bases although they pay more taxes than others which work in distinctive industries, therefore there is a balance within the people in what attracted with the rights and the national duties.

Each person receives the same treatment liquidated by the system to show so that it puts at national work. And that decreases the rate of crime, many time, people eat normally, exert their wills suitably and have access to entertainment. So they have stresses and they are to some extent delighted to be part of the system. And one thinks that everyone knows that misery gives birth to all distinct evils so that reign easily the usurper through the corners of that particular land.

All the principal described points exert by the state for the people. If the people can make the choice of his leaders, they can decide their manner of living. They will never make the choice of their failure, but of happiness.

In a word, the people are absolutely responsible to choose their leaders and the state itself also has its part in national scale.

The democracy is the part of demography and socialism is the fundamental base of many countries that maintain that formula.

Let's never forget that society forms of all demography in the panoramic phase thus inhabited whatever polyethnochromic or monoethnochromic.

Knowledge is the rail way which leads towards prosperity and it's also the most profound tool to fight misery!

Such the individual is worthy; much more the world needs him!

MISUSING OF THE
SOCIALIST SYSTEM

This elaborate formula is deceived by a great number of people who do not want to work seen that the system does not employ the strict means to detect them. In this case, many guys think that the government should push these people to work for the state or to go to school in order to learn a profession. If they refuse to do either one of them, the state should utilize another means to prevent their failure. The system encourages the people to become lazy, if it does not encourage them to work so as to reach the most standard in order to serve the country with their knowledge thus acquired. If somebody has the choice not to work, he limits himself and deceives the system which is largely opened to all. In fact, the perfect knowledge is the base which attaches to individual during his terrestrial race.

The screen shows that the tradesmen are victims the effect which they pay so much taxes when other ones take refuge in their beds.

This system is greatly appreciated by the ones which misuse it. But the ones which overload get tired by the unbalanced fact in the system. They would agree to help the handicap and old people, but not the ones who are able to do so. The national plans may continue to prevent the derailment of indulgence among the people in spite of deceiving by a great number of people. Certain governments choose to keep that good practice in order to help them.

A general freedom makes the demographic base is to learn any profession; the realization is that the rich person becomes richer because the wealth comes from his knowledge.

Many people do not appreciate what they have freely; they do for what they pay in that case, so the restructuration of that practice proves to be necessary.

The one which amuses to misuse the system makes sins against the state and the divine orders!

Let's get it right, who is able to get everything that he needs and makes the object to spend many years in school or writes down the theory that he receives from the source of science to make the technologies or philosophies available to all around the world?
Nobody!

FAILURE OF THE SOCIALIST SYSTEM

A weak system is effectively the concept of the foundation or the practice abused by the demographic class. If a partial of the population complaints against various abuses, the government should to some extent takes in fact measure to reorganize the system or requires a national conference for resolve the situation.

A failed system always brings a negative impact. It may depict unfortunately many aspects around the country like unbalance in the society, over-populated of the partial abused when the riches have less, hatred, laziness to work, going to school etc. So, this panoramic practice among the population should be restructured to adopt a new model. The Modern socialism is a systematic formula described as the optimal concept explaining reorganization to the traditional phase which certain people in the countries deceive this practice thus indicated.

In case the demographic refuses to decide, the state has to take an optimal decision.

An optimal decision would depict an optimal socialism that may center on the essential points which follow below:

1__The state imposes the wellbeing of the population.

2__Each individual inevitably has the right to put himself at work since it is a divine command, excluding the old and handicap people.

3__Annual taxes of each person around the territory.

4__Healthcare, each individual pays a value discussed monthly in the national scales; a value of 10% for each visit and the installation of preventive factors.

5__The state education ensured by the state, each graduated works one year period free for the state as a sign of gratitude.

6__The agriculture ensures by the state for a viable and autonomic economy.

7__The security completely ensures by the state as it is appropriate.

8__Each commercial part distinctively pays a relative tax based of the minimal or maximal value.

Sincerely, this splendid formula suggested would be greatly appreciated by the state and that the population would finally celebrate of that new prospect. This proposal is totally opposite to the traditional practice, but it would be for the happiness of all.

The good performance of the state indistinctly ensures each individual in the geographical framework.

That manner is a perfect work towards people which entrust the government this employment.

Reframing a weak system is not a sin, but letting go at derivative is a crime!

The driver ensures life of the travelers as long he keeps the railway that leads to their destiny!

Despite everything, this elaborated formula could be an effective mean which will help each individual so as to carry his part to develop the country and to enjoy suitably his independence. Even though, it does not reach the global monarchy of the transcendental elements coming from the heavenly place.

As long as the tree develops, circulates the sap!

COMMUNISM

There are the communist system and the communal practice of the primitive Christians:

The communist system imposes and which then generates socio dictatorial in certain territories to maintain it. Many countries which declare being Communists function against evolution or new technologies of all types. To retain captive people, the governments oblige to exert force or socio dictatorial on the population. There are two things to consider here: "the will of each individual and the one of dictatorship of each government" Only the etymological aspect or the practice could to some extent help to obtain the importance which claims the suitable order. Because missing the real context produces ignorance that leads to negative impact.

In a word, the countries which make the choice of communist system are pressed on the sticks or destructive weapons like dictatorship so as to endeavor their people to go to their liking to follow their ways involuntarily.

By finding a country which wants to practice this formula until arriving on a current scale according to the context of this topic is thus a disaster to be avoided. The population has to obey, not being able to retort the commands of that hardship government. This is why that the countries provided with this formula retain captive people until death. It is easy to say to others to practice the law, when the leaders themselves are excluded. The law does not exist for them, but well for other ones.

The leaders always like the power, daytime, they exert their power, in the night, and they think so as to increase on the population more law. The people of these governments are condemned to act according to the dictation of their chiefs. People cannot express their wills properly, but those of the socio dictatorial. If the creator gives will to the mankind, why are they detached from this privilege?

Indeed, one can to some extent realize that these governments commit crimes while thus acting

The point is that communist system according to the implication of the topic that spread certain leaders is also a social dictatorship by more sharp actions meaning system tallied established by somebody to endeavor the people to exert it, which indicates the population is under the dictation of somebody who controls. Thus there are a very great difference between the exercise of the primitive Christians and those which certain countries practice now. These two do not come from the same source and will never reach the same point.

The socio dictatorial which is placed easily destroyed the independence of territorial demography and it's a formula of slavery to attract on him the glances of all like the powerful whole. His mouth is largely open to pronounce his words, and people must have the ears largely opened to hear and obey without contradicting. The saved of this gangrene are the deaths ones. The living ones ask constantly, when will it be the day of their decease?

What everyone must know, when one cannot express what one wants, it is a boundary or a form of slavery, on this, one obtains the obviousness. Indeed, it is a system to avoid, because it makes suffering.

This formula is badly seen by the victims, but well by the sensualists.

The puffiness of the bees comes from the plants which the gardener under the blows of the sun cultivated!

The escaped ones can find death if they are founded by the government.

This formula is really a wild and timorous formula that partial of the earth into sudden unfortunately. People await a help to which being able to find by soft hearts of these chiefs or a governor coming to shake the ground by a tremor of high voltage for a total delivery.

People would say: when will come the day of their release?

The bad experiments remain vital in memory; but deliverance itself always comes from revolution which leads the brave ones to conquering!

If the way of living is our honor, this honor is already absorbed in the abyss. A new book of dictionary would write to place the words in the grammatical order, and then the word honor will get his position as it is appropriate. The word dishonor will also regain its place, so that the human beings will know and harmonize together. As the marvelous creature, God wants them to enjoy his splendor, his infinite love and his power continuously through the authentic world.

This system violates the precious orders and human right in substantial phases.

And it violates the willingness of each individual under its boots.

Communism retains in constraint, but the valiant ones always deviate from its railway yokes!

ITS NEGATIVE IMPACT ON FAMILY

The communist system retains the family in slavery. This systematic formula indeed destroys personality of each individual of the territory. By giving a standard of practice to people is a slave formula to exert in a constant way.

The husbands have in thoughts their chiefs as their dominators. They slightly occupy the second rank in the hearts of their wives.

The women equally obey the chiefs and splash in confusion. A constant unbalanced in the hearts of the couples which do not enjoy all the substances come from the matrimonial right. The right of preeminence is deserved only to the Master which controls universe. The children can resist the parents because they do not have full power to control them; even though these children are also slaves as of their birth.

This wild practice is not applicable animals, but usable on human race which should be reframed according the will of the population that gives the job to live a better way.

Someone hopes that this description thus will help men to advance deeply in knowledge to establish the difference between freedom and slavery which devalues them. Maintaining the truth to drain that mortal system is the guaranteeing the happiness of all.

The bluish liquid attracts the view, but its flavor destroys life!

COMMUNISM AND
EVOLUTION

With a sharp detail, one can perfectly discover the profound reality which gives access to develop so as to enjoy all substantial facts that come from this topic. This system is not applicable in this advanced world in order to keep humanity in progress. Communism would have to throw if it was existed in the global sphere.

This formula which prevents development also functions against life.

To avoid a catastrophe in the human society, evolution is better and preferable tool at the total base which ensures hope of all to advance from the scientific point of view by the new gradually ordered technological phases of the Master.

All products come from the scientific bases which are then used by men, for example: the planes utilized to travel of an extreme point to another extreme, boat, devices which go in space, telephones, nuclear bases, computers, Radio of communication etc. All new technologies or philosophies practical come from science that human beings rejoice. These devices that have been used by many people have an excellent utility. These factors by various philosophers exert the technological bases under the continual plan of God facilitating to humans, since he is the source of science.

Otherwise, all these facilities can surely neglect and which the world continues the first civilization or old that the men of formerly lived far from new technologies.

All countries must have to some extent access to technological faculties in order to meet the world challenges. Since the source of science gives in a gradual way, the preceding formula does not appreciate any more by the reduction of its value due to the new technologies coming from the abundant source. However, several countries see the things contrary.

According to the requirement of evolution, all the countries must advance on the rail's speed of development from prospect to new prospect.

Certain regime contrary terrace people so that it has all the vital bases around the geographical map by using agents as tool to destroy instead of making safe the population. It has every things for itself, its way makes tremble to retain its bad manner. It has all the Eastern points of the country; it crushes with its mortal shoes. It remains in its magnificence, while the people splash in misery without leaders and wait for help of an unknown being. This formula is like burning furnace to destroy. Is it a good preference to act with ferocity in order to reign in darkness?

Communism neglects the thoughts or message of the infinite source, the theory factor which other ones learn and technology or evolution like gradual production or the philosophical more advanced in physical matter base for the common utility of humanity to embellish and make prosperous while following the race under the powerful guide.

All scientific ways would be always remained hidden. The world needs exact knowledge, although received in a gradual way for happiness of all.

Indeed evolution or new technology is a preference for the moving world. The lesson is that the communist system is a destructive system, but evolution is constructive and shows the greatesss of that which sends the message, in spite of man thinks of occupying his place. This is why they are absolutely opposite.

The pathways of evolution are the best to illuminate human beings by new turnings that reshape the world!

Evolution leads on the track of new prospect, but communism removes the beauty of each individual and dishonors God by rejecting his transcendental commands!

Evolution is a structure implemented by God to embellish the human career of all scientific facts as a sign to show his magnificence and his infinite love!

What a favor!
What a splendid beauty!
What an infinite source for men of the authentic world!
"And each person is recommended of God to be put at work, and that which does not want to work proves that he has no right to eat"

Communism does not encourage the scientific aspects, such are the following:

1__Science of all branches

2__All theories of faculties

3__All technological or philosophical bases

This indicates, those which receive the messages coming from eternal God do not need to pay attention to it. The messages will not write to give access to others to know some. Technologies, physical phases or philosophical objects which use to give to students various faculties to carry a proper title on the matter indicated (philosopher).

Yes, if human systems which extend easily through all the earth do not manage to concretize absolutely what the Lord claims, it will cause an unfortunate consequence. It came the best moment to divert the path of defeat in order to gain what in conformity to his effective prescriptions.

This system is finally exerted against God's order and whole humanity in order to lead to world disaster.

FORMULA OF THE PRIMITIVE CHRISTIANS

World teaching would find the suitable object if each word utilizes according to its etymological context. The communal acts derived from the Greek word <u>Koinos</u> means share together, live together as a common agreement ``to voluntarily give, unconstrained" sharing mutually what they have."

Communal actions started with the primitive Christians when many of them did not have sufficiently the means of surviving of that time. As a sign of love, other believers put together voluntarily their wealth for helping, so that it does not have indulgence within the assembly. The latter were not imposed by well determined somebody, but they were acting voluntarily which means directly from their hearts. They had only one heart; they were blessed by God, the way in which they acted. This fact mentions in Acts chapter fourth according to the following verses 32-37; and Acts 2: 44-45. It was ended by the scattering of the people who lived outside, far from their native land.

The practice of the Christians did not have chance to extend around the world, by reading chapters 2 and 4 of the book of Acts, one is able to discover the exercises of the servants of Jesus and this practice ended by the dispersion of these believers, by persecution coming from the Jews.

If that formula exists again around the world, inevitably, it would right lead humanity to disaster. There is a very important factor to remember: when people get every things easily without working for or paying, they are not going to do nothing else, so that will surely lead to negative impact.

If it would be possible to extend through the terrestrial sphere, it would destroy all creation!

This formula is a border to the world evolution even though it appreciates by the observers and it also violates the ordering of the Master!

Obviously, it makes fatten the users, but the workmen have strong muscles to continue and the great honor for having access to enjoy their wealth!

DOES THE WORLD NEED THE COMMUNIST SYSTEM OR FORMULA OF THE PRIMITIVE CHRISTIANS?

Not at all, the world does not need the communist system and the formula of the primitive Christians; that imposed system exerts the dictatorship it is like metal fence, because it eliminates the will of each individual in the geographical framework. While operating under pressure of others is thus a violation whatever the plan. While the exercise of the primitive Christians retains people to take their responsibilities in a word encourages the idleness, fortunately this practice was stopped. The faculty of work is allowed the mankind to buy and sell in order to be able to fulfill the daily requirements of the human race.

Who wants to learn this great lesson from ants that are very small animals?

The ants' actions should push humanity to think in order to prove her superiority and her capacity!

Work is the fundamental base which leads to prosperity, independence and capacity on poverty!

Prosperity is the result that comes from work, but poverty is the disappointing dress of idleness whose friends are the givers!

This is why each person must put at work for better growing wealth. This system is in contradiction to evolution, it is like a defeat to have it. This failure system violates the human right and the Master's order of the Lord.

Indeed, this would be a disaster, if the communism was in fact extended around the world!

And the practice of primitive Christians will clearly lead to laziness!

However, one needs to remember that helping someone that splashes in bad situation is not the same like formula of the primitive Christians, they are totally different!

DEMOCRACY

Democracy is not a system, but the exerted civic or act of the people. The theme democracy comes from the Greek word <u>demokratos</u> made up of <u>demos</u> means people and <u>kratos</u> means law or rule, in a word: power or the civic exercise of the people. They can elect the best representatives at the various positions through all corners of the country in order to work in their liking suitably.

Many nations pretend providing this formula often do not delight, but the freedom or the popular power exists only at the time of the vote.

The right to vote is not enough definitively to supplement the topic which includes education, work, health, security and others. According to meaning of the word if democracy is to some extent the choice of the people while they suffer from all kinds of problems; that is a weak practice, because they would never choose to suffer. Thus let's imagine the people would never give the employment to somebody for better impoverishing.

One would need all the necessary elements which could supplement the democratic form, since misery raises all kinds of violence. And then, the representatives will move as enemies trying to establish peace among them, it is what occurs in many countries which are made believe that the democratic right is active. If the captains are unable to lead the boat, the population would have two ways of acting: leading or replacing the captains by other ones to bring the ship to the suitably intended port.

Finally, democracy is not a system, but definitively the power of the sovereign people!

TWO WORLD SHAPES OF SLAVES

These two shapes of slaves are the following ones:

1__SERVOPHYSIOLOGY
2__SERVOPSYCHOLOGY

SERVOPHYSIOLOGY

By using the factual etymology of this illustrated topic, one is able to describe in a sure knowledge dependently of the infinite source.

This theme is composed of three words, Servo means slave, Physio means physical: and logos means word or sturdy.

It's the scientific study of slave based on physical manner that contains various formulas practiced through the world which pushes oneself to make visible for the rise of mankind in what attracted at the restricted bases on these points which follow below.

1__The poor which delivers as slave to the rich just to make a living.

2__The one who works in full time under owner's order.

3__Other one that sold inside or outside their territory, continual factor nowadays in certain places.

1__The poor which delivers as slave to the rich person so as to make a living. He does not make a sin because he does not conceal. But deliver himself to a person as slave according to the meaning of the topic is to deny his natural being and to forget even his responsibilities.

His beauty exists in an invisible world because it is not easy to find in the planetary fields somebody who resembles to him although he is created with the resemblance to the living God. For him, leisure does not exist and he does not have an insurance to visit a doctor.

His social status does not have any value because it does not serve as nothing for him. One needs to know that the dominator often wanted a slave to work constantly. Sometimes the slave is whipping by the owner to have to forget to do something dependently his responsibilities. Certain people in this framework unfortunately undergo the erotic effect.

Slavery is not a profession, but a ruinous formula that many people profit!

2__ The one who works in full time under dictation of the employers.

Other one who works in full time always takes place at the request of his employer. The individual who delivers himself to work in this manner become slave, he forgets his wife, children, leisure and even oneself. This latter is a free slave, but the practice is a form of punishment.

However, the employer greatly appreciates him for being a good worker.

The woman and the children can devote themselves. And that can cause serious consequences by losing the woman and the children. She could be on the roof of a foreign ship at the sea-bed to discover a new planet contains various fruits, because the new experiments always eliminate the last ones which are already forgotten.

It is known that the family plays an extremely important part within each demography, although it is the smallest entity. When a member underwent a shock, other one suffers from the effect. While the slave cries, other guy is delighted and reigned. Can one call him king?

Believe it or not, he reigns! Let's not forget that many are these types of kings who are always ready to filling the vacuum and they are professionals which refuse to slow down. It is better to become slave of the family instead of becoming that of the different one. The case of confusing about the home address is sometimes the first pain in the hearth when empty is the family house.

That house undergoes of a tropical storm which carries all things and the queen, and leaving towards an unknown place. If it is impossible to dislodge the things, surely the queen would be gone. However, crying unceasingly never drives back the ocean, using wisdom is the best to avoid the unexpectable.

The children can wander many places, because the ploughed heart is not a victory, but a defeat. And they are often victims of the second rank after the uneven Father. If it would be possible to collect so many experiments, one would need thousands of years to gather them. This way of working does not bring joy, but of sorrow, it is better to have a piece of bread than having much in the path of suffering.

Being a free slave is also a form of spite. To be revoked from a job, nevertheless the house expects the arrival of the latter, but revoking from the house is like drying blood in the heart which announces the end. Using intelligence like a power and wealth is the existential base to triumph constantly.

It is a form based on the free slave. This composition is made appear in order to help the readers to better taking part in the world race normally.

To join to the modernization which requires effort, each individual must make intelligence the object of his constant practice.

The worker to apply to reality is given in kind to somebody according to his will, it is the shape of slave certainly, he goes home when he wants, but while being devoted to someone to exert his will is a kind of slavery. Work was given to men like a punishment after the disobedience of the first parents, and that becomes the duty to all men. It is true that work is the source of prosperity; this form is not a condemnation, but a divine duty.

The worker does not do it like a fun, but to make a living. One encourages to all to work as it is appropriate. All those which also put to serve others belong to this group of slaves.

Lastly, the realization is: to control or be useful, the controlled person is dominated, and the owner is the dominator.

3__Other one that sold inside or outside his territory is a continual factor nowadays in certain places.

This category is thus an old formula which continues in the various corners of the world which exceeds the conditions of the animals taking along to the slaughter-house. As a marvelous creature which lives to the manner of the scorned things.

This industry still develops in several corners of the earth. It seems that the owners do not give even a second to the slaves to breathe a little or does not look at them as beings of glory which deserve to be well treated. The slave of his tiredness would say: when would be the day of his death so that finally his body withdraws from immense flame and would even say that the days are too long.

However, the dominator would think that the years are too short, would even say that the man should live eternally. These years are not sufficient for the rich person to infinitely enjoy their wealth. The realization is that: it is better to be under the shade of the trees than of splash in slavery. The exercise of the quoted formula is not even applicable to animals. Who wants to delegate himself so as to help this world company to better treating slaves?

It would be an extraordinary action so that the latter know that eyes of the world observe all. The world should not close the eyes on the causes of the slaves. One hoped that this case will be in calendar of the new world order. And the great countries would see the need for defending this right fate of these slaves. And a new wind will blow as hope for the Western coast to release them. Then they would say, this planet does not miss one of those which live on it, a new smile would leave the hearts of the faces to make appear again their splendid beauty. This painful framework should not even be the subject of thoughts of the human race.

Not! It is inadmissible!

SERVOPSYCHOLOGY

It is composed of three words, Servo comes from the Latin word means slave, Psychos comes from the Greek word means mental or thought or dominated by: and logos comes from the Greek word means word.

In a word: it is the scientific study based on the shape of slave in the thought of a person dominated by:

Many people are accustomed to exerting this manner to blind others.

Servopsychology destroys the relationship between the human ones which based on mentality or thoughts, far from the profound reality. It is placed between two people, assemblies, industries and governments.

Individual that controls by other one becomes definitely his slave!

Delivering the heart to someone is to lead to his shaded continuation in the constraint whatever the distance. If someone controls the thoughts of an individual, he obtains that one and his wealth. If somebody offers his body without heart, he is a strong and independent guy.

The wise ones are powerful; one cannot gain them easily because they exceed the simple men!
Lead never controls by somebody, because this formula is condemned by the great Creator, one condemns it as well!

The intelligent man is well equipped with wisdom certainly to exert the amazing things. As far as it is advisable to advance valiantly to take care the mishaps!

The description given in the explored lines is the necessary tools which each individual must to some extent understand and practice constantly to hold firm like being especially created with the image of the heavenly Father.

These categories are defined in the etymological point of view for better informing the intellectual world of these structural phases in order to adapt on the speedway of the great civilization to arrive on the top of reality.

If somebody controls your mind, he also has all your being and your wealth!

THE DISTINCTIVE CIVILISATIONS THAT DEVELOP THE WORLD SYSTEMS AND THEIR SCIENTIFIC ASPECTS

Considering the great confusion which extends throughout the world the etymological details on topic 'civilization' can to some extent describe for a perfect comprehension and utility agreed upon for all; by stopping the deformation which is the subject of teaching by believing that the great countries are only ones civilized.

Civilization comes from the Greek word <u>politeuma</u> means condition or the practiced shape of people in a territory. Civilization is the way or condition living well defined people. Obviously, each country has its own civilization, the way of exerting.

The world is filled various forms of civilizations such are the following ones:

A__OLD CIVILIZATION
B__MODERN CIVILIZATION
C__ETHNO-PARALLEL CIVILIZATION
D__OPIMAL CIVILIZATION

OLD CIVILIZATION

The way of living after creation was the first civilization. A civilization is known as old when the population retains the same way in which the men at the end in certain corners of the earth exert, which do not need the scientific elements or new technologies. Inhabited in the forest, nourishing of fishing, hunting and plantations, they do not have the need for taking air plane, televisions, radios, computers, telephones, electricity and others. World information is not interesting to them, they are independents and they do not need service from other ethnics. They are controlled by themselves; they are detached from the rest of the world. They are proud to exert in their manner, and do not demand anything to others, because they are contemplated of a closed and distinguished circle.

These people, their manner practiced are their own civilization. They have a scorned formula of other people, and animals are the means of transport. Deprived of all scientific branches, despite everything they remain in joy, under the sun during the day and the moon facilitating by the luminous rays in the evening or stars. As under developed, they are happy practice of which they are useful. The unappreciated structures of houses are completely different to those of other populations. This figure although moved back and scorned developing countries. These people do not need the luxury of the world developed in scientific bases, and all these are the subject of their preferential independence.

In supplement, may this description helps to better understanding the topic.

In fact, each ethnic has his own civilization, his exerted or practiced manner!

MODERN CIVILIZATION

Modern civilization is the people of a development better than the old formula that containing the scientific necessary bases to fulfill the requirements which the world claims. A country which advances to new structures and that unemployment rate is minimized. The implementation respectively all the scientific systems which surround the country, the people which are not able to work receive a well defined treatment coming from the state.

Today, when one speaks about this formula, one lets see: the airlines and maritime routes function normally. The children attend the schools as appropriated, ensuring university of all students. An industrialized country facilitates people to be put at work progressively to reach new stages normally.

People who believe in the constant development, the national products of various species exported towards other countries contribute largely to enrichment. A population linked to conquer a quite specific thing always endeavors in order to achieve it. Increasing the new growths which indicate prosperity in prospect like ray for happiness, but the growth in decrease is the failure. Which people feel joyous of their failure? No one! That's why the developing countries still grow rich. The point is that modern civilization is one of the points which characterize the condition of well defined people.

In obviousness, each nation has her own civilization, the exerted or practiced manner.

ETHNO-PARALLEL CIVILIZATION

The word ethno comes from Greek language Ethnikos means ethnic of well defined

people that lived separately in a place concerned and detached of the great majority or mass.

The ethno-parallel civilization is an inhabited society in a broad demography of a country which retains her own manners of living like formerly.

It is an ethnic which keeps the manner of preparing the meals, keeping his own language, practicing his religion and habits etc.

These people, in spite of amusing of all privileges of the country, but they remain detached.

They use the better scientific bases in the majority although take part largely in the national development. This formula is not a phase which could push to revolt on, but accepting all although they are parallels in the demographic majority. They live in a foreign territory, but like living inside their territory. The thoughts of these people do not change; they are absolutely parallels to the large society.

Finally, this topic describes in a clear and simple way to increase the knowledge of all once and for all, because the real knowledge is a vital tool which indicates the right path to achieve the goal suitably.

Ethno-parallel civilization is really a separated society which retains the conditions of her country; it is a firm formula which cannot undergo any infiltration or influences of other ethnic ones. People remain unchangeable, jointing together between them, it is thus an ethnic subjected to all the patriotic phases, and exerting the sincere love which nourishes this incomparable unit. The children have to follow same works that the parents practice. It is a well organized population arming and persevering in the common practices; they feel happy to continue the same manners of living like free and independent people, as it is perfectly noted.

It is obvious that each nation has her own civilization, the manner of practice.

OPTIMAL CIVILIZATION

Optimal civilization is developed in richest and nation in the world; it is held on the top of the world pyramid. It is also more developed in industries and provide in sufficient means the products of good qualities than other nations, the food productions of any kinds are a continual viable phase which contributes to the richness of the nation while exporting outside the country, air routes are also a tangible facility by accomplishing voyages through inhabited planet.

It strongly brings a base contributing to the rich which allows the perfect and durable development. The sea routes play an extremely important part, exporting the merchandises towards other countries. Working in order to have the maximum scientific to satisfy and support others.

It's a population of highest level which means an optimal standard which achieves the goal in what attracted her vision.

This noble nation lives joyously, flourishing, powerful in all forms and right of respect. Her magnificence attracts other nations of the sphere to stare at on him as a sign of honor to experiment the highest civilization on a worldwide scale while considering.

These people have all the necessary things and even measure some to help others, population which has and retains this formula is the dominator of her ideas, moves from prospect to new prospect it is a formula to be imitated because it brings a source of happiness.

One may call it the world great power and is impossible to circumvent on the face of the earth.

It is a civilization which is held on the top of the world pyramid reaches the last step of the scale.

Which are the small ones to some extent which do not honor that giant of the world?

May the readers of the world are delighted for having access to this great opportunity. *Obviously, the great countries are not the only one civilized, but each country has its own civilization which is the manner of living.* Its luminous rays hope that the world endeavors to make reality the object of constant practices and remains strong. The right path guides to ensure the happiness of all without reserve.

This flourishing form is preferable and is the incomparable beauty which should always remain.

Optimal civilization is very advanced in technological or philosophical matters coming from the science.

One hopes that everyone knows that each nation whatever the demography has her own civilization, the manner of practice!

SCIENTIFIC ASPECTS FACE TO DISTINCTIVE CIVILIZATIONS OF THE WORLD

The scientific aspects depend completely on science coming from the Greek word 'gnosis' which means exact knowledge of the truth. It is the well defined field which gives a new direction to the human race.

For example: medicine is a scientific branch; theology is the scientific study of the word of God; sociology is the scientific study of the society. Science is composed of several disciplines. His multiple achievements help the men to get a better living; thus the time of Noah and the current era are completely different. The world is moved with the science which is extremely deep. It exists in an invisible way, but reproduces in the visible form and develops continuously. The sphere is filled with improvements due to science with the service of the humanity which is always delighted some. A scientific experiment is like a coarse basis at the beginning, but, progressively the formula changed and became more effective. It makes possible to travel in space to explore new planets, access to depth sea to make new discoveries. It managed to control energy to feed the various modern inventions like the telephone, cars, plane, boats and computer etc.

All these devices utilized by the men have an excellent utility. The enormous and fast ones need for the present time to prevent them from preserving the same forms since they are already curtailed. They must replace them by new structures. For this modernized world, the most modern are most eager out of progressive matters. An apparatus, for the same function, is appreciated only at the time of his invention. Once a new model arrives, the range and the width of the preceding one decrease. Their utility passes as from the memories when the instructive framework widens. All previous effects, today and tomorrow, are the subject of perfect happiness.

Science contains several opposite branches for different functions. Many effects are already discovered and others are not revealed yet. The knowledge of a given field is concretized gradually and is always moved. If one can make use of the productions of science, one proves her utilities to mankind. Each one of these branches has its own methods that explain the attachment with science. The scientific field is so vast that one will be able to never exhaust all the subjects.

SOURCE OF SCIENCE

From creation to the second dispensation, human beings splash in the old civilization. The great Creator makes them a manner to have access to do many things by spirit of intelligence. In the last dispensation or the great civilization, the living God gives faculty to the men of the earth to make extraordinary discoveries in order to think again about his existence and his faithfulness. If they are diverted of him to let mislead, they dishonor the Lord by saying that his marvelous things do not emanate from him, and they even deny that he created and that he has the capacity to operate all. Let's take one minute to think retrospectively on creation. The man does not have ease to operate actions of great scale as long as God does not authorize him to act. This is why in a visible way, one can build a computer of a well defined form this year, and in the following years one improves it.

God gradually gives what is called evolution of one until the infinite. One must realize that he gives it with measurement to the human ones, since one is absolutely under his dependence. He distributes the knowledge to which he wants, believer or unbeliever, even when each person did not receive same faculty according to his intention.

That which studies a specific field of the science and which professes this faculty continuously, receives a specific title according to his attachment with this discipline. Sociology is one of the branches of science. That which studies it calls: sociologist. Biology is also one of the branches of science; that which studies it calls: biologist. Of agreement or not, one must stress that there is only one truth. Without justification humans forget God and his marvelous works.

A__philosophy which denies that all knowledge comes from the eternal God; it is thus a heresy which presents a contradiction. It is easier to believe than the man comes from the worm of the earth or of a special animal and that will be appreciated of several. The things of this world become idols. If the men receive glory in the place of the great Creator, one is in a deep sleep. The world is on reverse because of his behavior. Now, reality is well put in function for the best.

One can accept that the man is one of the creatures of God who put in his body the spirit of intelligence to reveal the plan of the Lord. All scientific facts discovered by human coming from the source of all obvious knowledge. Modernization of all times implies that which devotes to science does not make it or give it once and at all. Let's not forget that the omniscient God is the source of science.

Truly, God is the source of science that does many and amazing things in favor of human beings that he created according to his perfect image, but not to animals which live without spirit of intelligence!

Science booms in space its powerful glares, so humans grab and rejoice the technologies that transform the world!

The last dispensation is absolutely the field of evolution that depicts a new world to manage which grab easily by the young ones, but remains a great challenge for many old ones!

Technologies are the effective products that transform human beings in a greater way for a new standard of living!

The scientific aspects invade the world to regroup the nations in one society in order to be closed; therefore, the closer they are, the better they'll feel!

SCIENCE AND
TECHNOLOGY

The scientific structures are described as follows:

1__the thought or invisibility first of the scientific phases.

2__the theory or literal philosophy

3__the physical or concrete partial.

A__the thought or invisibility depends directly on God. The hidden things are with him, but the revealed things are to human beings.

B__the theory or literal philosophy is the written data, coming from the spirit of intelligence that one teaches to the men before the physical application or the visible manner is thus the second phase.

C__the physical phase or concrete partial is the visible base of the field being put at the work by the men. The person to whom this faculty is allotted receives a well defined title. Other ones are delighted by this fact and glorified the great Creator of all.

It is the right sign of the faithfulness of the living God to perverse humanity.

Indeed, each individual should discover that God is the source of science!

Science leads to progress, but ignorance degrades and directs to defeat!

PHILOSOPHICAL OR TECHNOLOGICAL STRUCTURES

Philosophy comes from two Greek words (phileo) which means like or love and (sophia): means wisdom or knowledge from reality; it is defined as the love of wisdom or knowledge based on reality. Any structure which known as philosophical contrary to reality is a perverse form. Philosophy or technology is not a means to be diverted, but to progress. The way, in which one uses it, it's not well defined. The cells which must be the object of utility for the men loosing value gradually. Is it not the time to reconsider the right track? By pointing out that philosophy or real technology is the product of the science which the new formulas always replace.

A fact is known as philosophical point when its structure is the scientific base. It is a branch of the science perfectly exerted by the individual.

And a philosopher is that which likes a branch that he receives training for and practices that wisdom or knowledge; that one which does not practice the knowledge coming from the truth is not philosopher. Must of them do not want to believe that God is the only source of science and then, they want to be called philosophers. Today, the light is shining to guide on the real pathway for a long time of intense confusion. One wants to contribute in order to find a clearness that pushes to seek the meaning of a word, because each topic has its own definition. The weight of the lie decreases gradually until even disappearing in the scale balance, but that of the truth always remains. It is hoped that this theory will be appreciated to be usefully.

Philosophy or technology is the fact that the human ones always use, and it is not a surprise, but a fundamental reality.

Technologies shown evolution and civilization electrified the knots!

VARIOUS ASPECTS OF PHILOSOPHY

These aspects are the following:

a) The primitive philosophies which are null and void in what attracted the evolution coming from science. Their manners insufficiencies show clearly the failure when it is a question of enclosing the new invoices;

b) The practical philosophies are usually applied to the gradual technological facts of science and humanity follows the new prospect;

c) The subversive theories constitute the tricks of the usurper to combine the real and bad things together, so as to falsify the theories emanating of the infinite source, and to destroy the plan of the Master by confusion so that he is not glorify through the transcendental theories. This is why many people do not want to give honor to the Master who operates marvelous things gradually. The Lord does not give his glory to angels even to perverse men.

The child throws away the treasury that the explorer grabs!

SCIENTIFIC TRANSITIONS

Science is the mother of all the technological or philosophical branches gradually given from the Lord, source of all scientific objects that humans use, show in fact the faithfulness of the great Creator of the universe.

The individual who receives from the source the theory, sees already the object, but the technology which the philosophers or technicians build that human beings utilize greatly.

The transition is described as followed:

1__God
2__professors
3__philosophers or technicians
4__technologies or philosophies

A__ the almighty God is the source of the science which gives it in a gradual way to human beings until the destruction of all creation.

B__ the professors are those which receive the order or the message or the theory of God without mixture and which is then the object to teach to people who love that discipline so much in order to be ready to serve other ones; one calls them inventions that have invented the scientific factors.

One has just announced that the mention of scientists and several sciences is a serious error in the world teaching. If reality shed the tears of the students for a little time, soon, the joy will be their crown to triumph!

Let's not forget that the scientists and several sciences do not exist.

But they are professors or philosophers or technicians; and different branches of scientific productions.

Remember, there is only one science which produces many scientific branches.

C__ the philosophers or technicians are those which like so much this technological formula while becoming as students to learn the theory which indicates the formation of the object or the technique. They received formation technological matter or philosophical in that particular matter for better serving others. They must be open to follow the new decisions of the infinite source which can in made change the objects which follow the information relatively. They must be ready in case which the Master decides to maintain the form in a power more advanced for better getting informed about the theory added in order to be up to date.

D__ All the scientific branches are the philosophical or technological elements used everywhere come from the science whose God is the source. There exists only one science, but there are a variety of scientific branches, technological or philosophical ones that humans for an excessive and advanced world which has been operated gradually.

The Master granted it, the world grabbed it!

Certain countries vis-à-vis technologies are detached absolutely from the world.

Although God utilizes anyone he wants at any place. The messengers who receive the order cannot in fact continue or bring the theories because they do not have the means of production. Like countries under developed, they continue their old career.

The countries of great civilizations by the means of production advance technologies in new technologies gradually. They can conquer theories in the countries that are not developed for better growing rich.

These same scientific devices being the subject of utility where the theories come that the people delight.

All countries have the need for developing out of technological matter so as to be ready to face the requirements of the modern world.

The things discovered on the earth, in the earth and the air do not form part of the facts known as scientific, but of discoveries.

Science does not come from the earth, but from the heavenly Father!

There is a great confusion around the world in what attracted the theme of science. However, this fundamental topic is absolutely the gradual knowledge coming from God. Spirit of intelligence which transmits the message or knowledge distinctive to soul of the particular individual to put in execution the object or the Master's order according a specific theory for the world greater utilities comparing to the former times.

The fundamental fact is to realize that the theme science is the decision of God carries out to human beings by spirit which establishes the difference between them and other creatures.

The implication is that all factors scientifically humans used before, today and tomorrow are clearly the productions reveal by spirit of intelligence coming from the infinite source.

Spirit leads the effective facts of science by the ruling theories, even though it remains a real challenge for many people in the world!

EPILOGUE

Finally, the screen depicts the human systems completely, their scientific civilizations and their points indistinctly to enrich all the explorers around the world. Certain human systems throw the men in the most intense desolation.

And one of them is instituted at the end of times, global monarchy; however it is thus an intimate business between humanity and the Master in what attracted with salvation.

Many do not want to abolish the formulas which make suffering the people to be able to maintain the weak ones in slavery. All the formulas of the world which function against the will of the people should put in reorganization before directing to disaster.

It is absolutely a clear signal for the men of the authentic world to move towards a new prospect.

It is extremely impossible to deny the authenticity and the importance of the people created with the image of the Master who gives the same value to each one.

This is why he continues to make shine knowledge at the end of times by gradually advanced technological phases for the happiness of all men in all places.

Although the elements which are in the global system of God do not find in the whole of the human systems, they are not consisted by the same factors. What implies the systems of the men are not identical to that of the Master who wants that his order exerts on all men. That must draw the attention of all for a world mobilization in order to reject all the painful practices which make suffering so as to conquer the best.

Certainly, a world conference to discuss on these fundamental points would be necessary in order to put a term at this total crisis.

Alternative of time suggested to human beings of the authentic world!

The Father has been waiting for the willingness acts of all as signs of a mission implemented by humans. With the demographic framework selecting by God through the terrestrial sphere among all those which breathe. He extends his plan of love to show his responsibilities to the men so much suitable at the end of times, why not among the human ones.

One should not deposit the load on the shoulders of others which have of the same privilege like oneself. Each individual must mobilize himself for the implementation of a better system, and that the light will shine on the terrestrial sphere and the intensity of heat on the sphere will decrease like tangible signs which presents on the world screen the preparation to seize durable happiness. Never forget that the exerted manner will determine the misfortune or happiness.

The world systematic graphs absolutely depict a muddled spectacle. They are parallel to global monarchy and they're presented a disorder within the global demography.

The panoramic distinctions that the systems of the world present require finally a reorganization to regain the best.

It is an incomparable system which has a common treatment for each individual around the world.

Due the world is being filled of various systems, which among them do you prefer?

The axis of the untiring explorers of the authentic world!

The graph depicts the establishment of the unbalanced systems which raised confusion around the world. However, a minimal number in the total demography around the sphere is still holding a tight knot. Nowadays, it's extremely important that the world's jury examines impartially the obviousness in order to pronounce his verdict!

ABOUT THE AUTHOR

I was born in Saint-Marc, Haiti on June 7th, 1961. The child of Alexis Jadis and Clercine Dieujuste. I made my primary studies in the countryside, and my secondary studies in my birthplace.

In 1981, I made the best choice by accepting Jesus as my personal Savior. I was twenty years old when I thought of becoming the son of the living God, by taking an active part as member of a church in conformity with the proper doctrine of this assembly.

It was the Friday May first 1981 at 5 p.m. of afterwards midday. I was looking for the truth. It is imperative to all those which seek God to sacrifice for the best which is not elsewhere and to fight to make shine the divine and absolute truth.

In 1984, I have privilege to marry with my preferred young girl. After the birth of elder one, I had the privilege to travel in Turks and Caicos Islands and to turn over to my country to continue the family's race.

I continued to work conscientiously in assembly of which I formed part. As of the year 1987, the Almighty Lord sent on my road somebody which knew perfectly my will to find the truth. He addressed questions to me which I did not dare to answer:

This preacher encouraged me to read the following verses: Matthew 16, 18; John 3, 5; 1 Corinthians 3, 11; 1 Corinthians 15, 1-2 and others. After these readings, I realized in a manner understandable that the path was traced right in front of me to undertake the Christian race in order to reach the goal which already my heart wished. I was integrated in the spiritual kingdom of Christ by the baptism in obedience of the Gospel in which I had access. I received forgiveness of my sins by the Holy Spirit which marks the presence of God in my current career in order to be able to maintain the model of Jesus and to prepare to meet this powerful Savior for his apparition.

I took part in a following seminar after my conversion to be able to enrich by adequate spiritual knowledge, for a suitable spiritual growth under the power of the heavenly Father. This seminar was animated by various teachers from many nations, the advancing framework and redemptive mission of Christ. After the graduation, I engaged firmly in this glorious framework under the control of the Holy Spirit to teach the salvation plan of the Lord.

During years 1987-1989, I worked as brother of the church, founder and director of a community school supporting by Minister Emmanuel Alexandre.

I had the privilege to found many associations through various localities. I became the coordinator of these associations thus founded. Teaching by Father Gerard and Renaud Bernardin in fact to help people to organize themselves to maintain their civil rights and duties as it is appropriate. And helping in unity at the base of durable development that leads to prosperity. Despite the difficulties, but the will pushed me to carry my contribution to various unfolding which could lead to the top of their destiny.

At the end of the year 1989, for better encouraging them, I have the privilege to take part in the electoral competitions, precisely the town hall of Marchand Dessalines in December 16th, 1990.

I was greatly misled, because the opponents at the time destroy the aspirations of the people by relieving the elected president by a blow of military. And 75% of the elected officials threw outside to escape of tortures coming from the latter which extended through all corners of the country.

That indicates that the willingness does not always express provide as indicated. Following the painful situation which knew the country, I was obliged to travel to the United States of America. In New Jersey, of 1993-1996, I learned English to be able to integrate in the new carrier. With the rigor of the climate in this State of North, my family and I made the decision to move to Florida. We've been there since June 1996. As servant of the Lord, I want to bear my responsibility to preach the gospel, the good news of Christ by putting this work at the range of all as a sharp richness which humanity needs for the happy life.

Graduated, in the scientific faculty of branch of theology in order to contribute carefully to the teaching of the marvelous framework for a possible evolution under glance of the great Architect of the universe, in order to widen the divine mission through the whole world to regain the treasury given up for a perfect happiness.

At the beginning of the year 1998, I contributed to work in American church of Christ in Orlando Florida as evangelist at this particular assembly until the end of the year 2003. Since January 2004, I am held to work as leader of the church of Christ to achieve the intention of God of glory.

I want absolutely to engage in this valuable world mission to proclaim the deliberation suitably in the whole humanity which loses her right and gives up her duty, and which cannot deny itself as the higher creature among others for a well defined reason. A recall comes from the Master before the very last catastrophe in order to arrive to the possible reality to circumvent of which I am the subject of my application. Since the heavenly vocation demands it, an irresistible implication as devoted missionary by keeping the faithfulness.

Continuity of the creative work lets see again that a birth is always an amazing thing that should precede of honor and glory to the living God, the great Creator and Master of the universe!

Man of the authentic world!